MYTHOLOGY AND CULTURE

WHAT WE GET FROM GREEK MYTHOLOGY

KATHERINE KRIEG

Published in the United States of America
by Cherry Lake Publishing
Ann Arbor, Michigan
www.cherrylakepublishing.com

Consultant: Thomas Keith, Instructor, Liberal Arts, School of the Art Institute of Chicago; Marla Conn, ReadAbility, Inc.
Editorial direction and book production: Red Line Editorial

Photo Credits: Shutterstock Images, cover, 1, 7; National Geographic Society/Corbis, 5; Georgios Alexandris/Shutterstock Images, 8; David Lees/Corbis, 11; Christie's Images/Corbis, 14; US Navy, 17; Public Domain, 18 (left); Elaine Thompson/ AP Images, 18 (right); NASA, 19; Andreas Praefcke, 21; Sorin Colac/Shutterstock Images, 23; Everett Collection, 25; Kerry Brown/Paramount/Everett Collection, 26 (top); Buena Vista Pictures/Everett Collection, 26 (bottom); Eriko Sugita/ Reuters/Corbis, 27; Fox 2000 Pictures/Everett Collection, 28

Library of Congress Cataloging-in-Publication Data

Krieg, Katherine, author.
  What we get from Greek mythology / by Katherine Krieg.
    pages cm. -- (Mythology and culture)
  Includes index.
   ISBN 978-1-63188-913-4 (hardcover : alk. paper) -- ISBN 978-1-63188-929-5 (pbk. : alk. paper) -- ISBN 978-1-63188-945-5
(pdf) -- ISBN 978-1-63188-961-5 (hosted ebook)
  1. Mythology, Greek--Juvenile literature. 2. Civilization--Greek influences--Juvenile literature. 3. Greece--Civilization--
Juvenile literature. I. Title.

BL783.K75 2015
398.2ʾ0938--dc23

                            2014029990

Cherry Lake Publishing would like to acknowledge the work of
The Partnership for 21st Century Skills. Please visit www.p21.org
for more information.

Printed in the United States of America
Corporate Graphics
December 2014

ABOUT THE AUTHOR

Katherine Krieg is the author of many books for young people. She has been interested in Greek mythology since reading the *Iliad* when she was 15 years old.

TABLE OF CONTENTS

CHAPTER 1

The Great Greeks

You may not be aware of it, but you have probably heard of many Greek gods. Their names have been reused for many purposes in **modern** culture. Nike shoes are named after the Greek goddess of victory. The planet Uranus is named after the Greek god of the sky. There are even popular sports teams named after powerful Greek gods. The Greeks worshiped these gods thousands of years ago. But many of their names are still familiar to us today.

Records of people living in Greece date back to
6000 BCE. Most of Greece's contributions to the modern
world come from a time known as the classical period.

The ancient Greeks' culture flourished thousands of years ago, but their mythology still affects us today.

This stage of Greek history lasted from approximately 500 BCE to 330 BCE.

During this period, the thriving city of Athens was the center of Greek culture. Athens was the first city to develop a **democracy**. In a democracy, citizens have a say in how their government works and who their leaders are. This political system is still used by the United States and many other countries. However, democracy in ancient Athens was restricted to adult male citizens. Slaves, foreigners, and women were not allowed to participate.

In Athens and most other parts of the ancient world, people were **polytheistic**. This means that they worshiped multiple gods. Greeks believed that their gods lived atop Mount Olympus. They believed the gods looked like humans but had magical, superhuman powers. The gods sometimes fought with each other.

The ancient Greeks were interested in understanding the world around them. If they could not explain

The ruins of ancient Athens still stand in the middle of the modern city today.

something they saw in nature, they often believed the gods caused it. For example, they believed that the god Zeus caused thunderstorms when he was angry.

In some Greek myths, the gods interacted directly with humans. The poet Homer wrote down two of these stories, the *Iliad* and the *Odyssey*, approximately 2,800 years ago. Before they were written, the stories passed

Mount Olympus is the tallest mountain in Greece.

from generation to generation as people told them aloud. People continue to enjoy these two epic poems today.

Although much of ancient Greece is now in ruins, its mythology lives on in our modern culture. Much of the world's art, architecture, literature, and popular media have been deeply influenced by the ancient Greeks.

GO DEEPER

CAREFULLY REREAD THIS CHAPTER. PICK OUT A MAIN POINT THE AUTHOR IS TRYING TO MAKE. WHAT EVIDENCE CAN YOU FIND FOR THIS POINT?

Many Gods

In Greek mythology, there were several major sets of gods. Two of the most important were the Titans and the Olympians. The Titans were a group of elder gods who ruled the earth before the Olympians did. The god Cronus led the Titans. Cronus tried to eat all of his children so that none of them would grow up and **overthrow** him.

Cronus's wife, Rhea, was devastated that all her children were being eaten. She tricked Cronus into swallowing a rock instead of eating their new baby,

One of the Titans, Atlas, was said to have held the world on his shoulders.

Zeus. As a result, Zeus was able to grow up and overthrow his father. Zeus also made Cronus vomit up the rest of Zeus's siblings. Zeus then became king of the new gods, the Olympians.

There were 12 Olympian gods. These gods represented different themes and had different powers. They are called the Olympian gods because they were believed to live on Mount Olympus.

Greek mythology featured many other lesser gods as well. Many of them were related to each other. The gods were not always wise and **moral**. They made mistakes

Major Greek Gods

Aphrodite	Goddess of Beauty and Love
Apollo	God of Light, Music, and Prophecy
Ares	God of War
Artemis	Goddess of Hunting
Athena	Goddess of War and Wisdom
Hades	God of the Dead
Hephaestus	God of Fire
Hera	Queen of the Gods, Goddess of Marriage
Hermes	Messenger of the Gods
Hestia	Goddess of the Home
Poseidon	God of the Sea
Zeus	King of the Gods, God of Thunder and Storms

[21st Century Skills Library]

and sometimes behaved badly toward each other and toward humans. Some characters in Greek myths had one human parent and one parent who was a god. These characters often lived on Earth but still had some godly powers.

In addition to the gods and half gods, Greek mythology is filled with terrifying creatures. One such creature was the Hydra. The Hydra was a **serpent** that breathed out poison and had multiple heads. If one head was cut off, the terrible monster grew two more in its place. Another creature was the Chimera. This animal had the body and head of a lion, but it had a snake for a tail and a goat's head attached to its back. In Greek mythology, a Chimera sighting meant that a bad storm might soon occur.

There are many different sources of Greek myths. The best-known stories come from the *Iliad* and the *Odyssey*. The *Iliad* is a story about the Trojan War, which archaeologists believe may have been a real war between

The Trojan War involved many gods and legendary Greek heroes.

the Greeks and the Trojans. The Trojans lived in Troy, a city in present-day Turkey. In the story, the gods got involved in the battle, often stepping in to help the fighting warriors.

The *Odyssey* takes place after the Trojan War, following the events of the *Iliad*. It describes the story of the Greek hero Odysseus as he overcomes obstacles on his journey back home after the war. The *Odyssey* includes a reference to the Trojan horse, which is still familiar to many people today. In the story, the Greeks give the Trojans a giant wooden horse as a gift during the war. When the Trojans take the gift into their walled city, Greek soldiers climb out of the horse and destroy the city.

The gods play a part in the story of the *Odyssey*. The gods Athena and Zeus take pity on Odysseus and help him get home. With the help of the gods and his own determination, Odysseus makes it home to his family. Much like popular stories of today, Greek mythology is full of conflict and drama.

THINK ABOUT IT
DISCUSS THIS CHAPTER WITH A CLASSMATE. WERE ANY OF THE STORIES FROM GREEK MYTHOLOGY FAMILIAR TO YOU? WHERE HAD YOU HEARD THEM BEFORE?

A UNIVERSE OF INFLUENCE

Greek mythology and culture have had major impacts on today's culture. From city names to space exploration, Greek mythology has been influential in many areas of culture.

In the United States, words from Greek mythology have become the names of many cities. Athens, Georgia, was named after Athens, the capital city of Greece. The name comes from the goddess Athena. There are also U.S. cities named after Ares, Apollo, Hades, and many

The U.S. Navy's Aegis system uses fast, accurate missiles to shoot down enemy missiles.

other Greek gods. Sports teams, such as the Tennessee Titans, also take their names from Greek mythology.

Numerous companies in the United States have looked to Greek mythology for inspiration. Ajax is the name of a hero in the *Iliad* and is now the name of a cleaning product. In Greek mythology, Zeus and Athena used a shield called the Aegis. Today, Aegis is the name of an insurance company. The U.S. Navy also uses the name Aegis for a system that defends ships from missile attacks.

LOOK AGAIN

Take a look at this image of the Greek Titan Oceanus, left, and a Tennessee Titans football player, right. Why might a football team want to be named after the Titans?

The United States borrowed Apollo's name for its program that sent people to the moon.

Greek mythology has even reached the far corners of space. Moons, **asteroids**, and satellites are named after places or characters from Greek myths. For example, one of Pluto's moons is named Kerberos, which is a three-headed dog that lived in the **underworld** according to Greek mythology. In the 1960s, the U.S. plan to land people on the moon was named Project Apollo after the Greek god of light. From everyday products to outer space, influences from Greek mythology can still be seen today.

CHAPTER 4

EVERYDAY WORDS, FAMOUS BUILDINGS

Have you ever been furious with your friend? On a steamy summer day, have you ever heard someone say, "It's hot as Hades!"? Have you ever seen a house or building with large columns in the front? You may not realize it, but some of the language and architecture that is part of your everyday life comes directly from Greek mythology and culture.

Many English words originated in ancient Greece. Some of the words have direct ties to the Greek myths. For example, the word *fate*, meaning one's destiny or

The three Fates were often depicted as three women in robes.

future, comes from the Latin word for the Fates, characters in Greek mythology. The Fates decided when a person would die. *Fury*, meaning extreme anger or violence, is another word related to a myth. In Greek mythology, Furies were creatures that tormented people who had committed murder.

Many popular phrases also come from Greek myths. The phrase "hot as Hades" refers to the god Hades, who ruled the underworld. You may also have heard the phrase "Achilles's heel," which is a person's weak spot. In Greek mythology, Achilles was a hero with a goddess mother and a **mortal** father. When Achilles was a baby, his mother dipped him in the River Styx, the boundary between the underworld and Earth. This protected Achilles's body from harm. However, the part of his heel where his mother held him did not touch the water. Achilles eventually died when an arrow pierced his unprotected heel.

It is very likely that you've seen buildings inspired by ancient Greece many times in your life. Perhaps the most famous ancient Greek building is the Parthenon, a temple in Athens, Greece. It was dedicated to the goddess Athena. The columns that make up the sides of the temple are common in Greek buildings and are still used all around the world today. Many of the buildings in Washington, DC, are modeled after this type of Greek architecture. There is also a replica of the Parthenon in Nashville, Tennessee. The ancient Greeks left a beautiful legacy of language and architecture that is still familiar to us today.

LOOK AGAIN

LOOK CAREFULLY AT THIS PHOTO. DOES IT REMIND YOU OF ANY BUILDINGS YOU'VE SEEN?

GODS AS MOVIE STARS

Many of the stories and characters described in this book may already be familiar to you through movies or books. These stories have endured for centuries, although they may have different forms in the modern world.

There are several instances of Greek mythology in animated Disney films. Disney's *Fantasia* has a **segment** that features many of the Greek gods, including Zeus and Apollo. The movie *Hercules* tells the story of the Greek hero Hercules, also known by his original Greek name Heracles. He is half-human and half-god. In the film, Hercules faces off against Hades. However, the film shares only a few things in common with the actual myths.

Hercules has been a popular subject of films since the days of black-and-white movies.

LOOK AGAIN

TAKE A LOOK AT THESE TWO IMAGES OF DIFFERENT VERSIONS OF HERCULES. WHICH DO YOU THINK LOOKS MORE LIKE THE HERCULES THE GREEKS TOLD STORIES ABOUT?

Brad Pitt starred as Achilles in the film Troy.

There are many other live-action movies focused on Greek myths. In 2004, *Troy*, starring Brad Pitt as Achilles, turned the *Iliad* into an action movie. There are several movies that deal with Olympian gods and Greek heroes, including *Clash of the Titans* and its sequel, *Wrath of the Titans.*

The Percy Jackson books, based on Greek mythology, were also adapted into a series of movies.

[21ST CENTURY SKILLS LIBRARY]

Author Rick Riordan's Percy Jackson and the Olympians series of books features a modern take on Greek myths and characters. In the books, a boy named Percy Jackson discovers that he is a son of Poseidon, the Greek god of the sea. Jackson and his friends travel to the River Styx, search for Zeus's lightning bolt, and meet Hades.

Although Greek mythology may seem like a thing of the past, it continues on. Your everyday life is affected by this ancient civilization, from the words you speak to the movies you watch. The legacy of ancient Greek culture lives on all around the world.

THINK ABOUT IT

WHAT DO YOU THINK THE ANCIENT GREEKS WOULD THINK ABOUT THE MOVIE VERSIONS OF THEIR MYTHOLOGY? WOULD THE STORIES SEEM FAMILIAR TO THEM, OR TOTALLY DIFFERENT? DISCUSS THESE QUESTIONS WITH A CLASSMATE.

THINK ABOUT IT

- In Chapter One, you learned about ancient Greece. Why do you think so many stories came out of this time period? How did the way people lived affect their beliefs?

- Find a reliable Web site about Greek mythology. Can you find different versions of the myths or different descriptions of the characters? Why do you think these differences exist?

- What is the most surprising way Greek mythology and culture affects your life today? Why is it so surprising to you?

LEARN MORE

FURTHER READING

Evans, Lady Hestia. *The Mythology Handbook: A Course in Ancient Greek Myths.* New York: Candlewick, 2009.

Jennings, Ken. *Greek Mythology.* New York: Little Simon, 2014.

Napoli, Donna Jo. *Treasury of Greek Mythology: Classic Stories of Gods, Goddesses, Heroes & Monsters.* Washington, DC: National Geographic, 2011.

WEB SITES

National Geographic Kids: Tales of Terror from Ancient Greece!
http://www.ngkids.co.uk/did-you-know/Greek-Myths
This Web site features stories and illustrations from Greek mythology.

Primary History Ancient Greeks: Gods and Heroes
http://www.bbc.co.uk/schools/primaryhistory/ancient_greeks/gods_and_heroes
Read this Web site to learn more about Greek gods, temples, and heroes.

GLOSSARY

asteroids (ASS-tuh-roidz) small rocks traveling in the Sun's orbit

democracy (di-MOK-ruh-see) a system of government in which leaders are elected by the citizens

modern (MOD-urn) something in recent times

moral (MOR-uhl) concerned with doing the right or correct thing

mortal (MOR-tuhl) a human

overthrow (oh-vur-THROH) to force out of power

polytheistic (pol-ee-thee-ISS-tic) to believe in or worship more than one god

segment (SEG-muhnt) a part

serpent (SUR-puhnt) a large snake

underworld (UHN-dur-wurld) a land of the dead

INDEX